A Summer Job

Valsetz, Oregon 1951

DUDLEY COLLARD

D'Oc Publishing

D'Oc Publishing, LLC
PO Box 564
Lake Park, GA 31636

This book is a memoir.

Cover Design: Lisa Buie-Collard
All Drawings: Dudley Collard

ISBN: 978-0-9836478-6-7
Library of Congress Control Number: 2016933587
D'Oc Publishing, LLC, Lake Park, GA

To the memory of the Valsetz millworkers.

INTRODUCTION

The following account of my summer in 1951, working for the Valsetz Lumber Company, in the no longer extant town of Valsetz, Oregon, was written in the early 1960s. I felt that I would like to put down my recollections of what was, to me, an unique experience, before either I forgot them, or worse, began to 'embroider' them in order to make a better story.

Valsetz was a company town up in the middle of the Coast Range, some 40 miles by road west of Salem. All life in the town revolved around the mill whistle, whether it was to start the day or to end it.

The mill lay on the edge of a large artificial lake (the mill pond), which drained towards the Pacific Ocean, but both the road and the company railroad came up to it from the Willamette Valley. The town was surrounded and dominated by the very rough Coast Range terrain, all covered with small growth, having been longed off a long time before. The mill was fed by timber cut further away up in the mountains.

The summer of 1951 was very hot and dry and there was a continual worry that logging in the powder dry woods would have to stop. Every day the level of humidity was anxiously discussed. As I remember, if the level dropped below 4 percent in the woods it was "All Out!", but if logging did stop for a short while the mill kept going all the time that I was there.

Having been taken on knowing absolutely nothing I could only learn, and at Valsetz I learnt a lot.

Over 60 years later I remain grateful at the way my fellow workers accepted me and helped me. Stan Henry, a great character and my boss and mentor throughout much of the summer, would be most surprised to know that one of the lessons that he gave to the callow college boy "English," or was it "Slim?" (and it was a lesson) would one day be used to help me modify part of the wing of the Concorde supersonic airliner!

Valsetz Lumber Mill 1951

The mill was old, and it was considered by the men to be a bit unsafe. In a few years the timber would be gone from the region and the management didn't seem to consider it worthwhile to replace old and dangerous machinery. In the summer of 1951 however, I only saw two accidents and although both were hospital cases, no one was killed.

The father of a friend of mine, Mr. Skoboe, had worked there as a millwright the year before and he wrote me a letter of introduction to the superintendent Mr. Brownjohn. Of course, although the letter was written to Mister Brownjohn he was referred to simply as "Brownjohn," which I took to be Brown John. I thought that he must be at least half Indian.

To work in the lumber industry in Oregon, State Law said that you had to be at least eighteen years old. This age could easily be checked by the company doctor by his asking for your Selective Service draft card. If you were under eighteen you had to find a solution.

I was seventeen and I had emigrated to the U.S.A. two years earlier. My parents had bought a nice blue 1940 Dodge sedan that spring (for $500) and they said that they could drive me to Valsetz. None of my friends had a car sufficiently reliable to guaranty getting there. So I accepted being driven there in the Dodge although it did cross my mind that it was not liable to improve my chances of getting a job if it was seen that "Daddy and Mummy" had driven me there and were waiting anxiously outside the mill office to learn of my success or otherwise. To get to Valsetz you could drive down 99W through McMinnville and Amity to Rickreall, and take the turning to Dallas. From Dallas you drove up to the remnants of Falls City where the road apparently ended.

There was only one street in Falls City, with some sorts of ware-houses or shops and a couple of saloons. Above the town there may have been a few houses. The "City" ended abruptly at the "Falls," but just before arriving at the garbage dump and the beginning of the woods a dirt road to the left crossed over a wooden bridge and climbed away up the side of the mountain. This was the road to Valsetz. It was about one truck width wide over most of its length and was dirt for the seventeen miles into the mill, except where it was bulldozed down to bedrock. I have never seen an official map of the region but "up 3000 feet and down 1400 feet, with over 300 bends" sticks in my mind.

It was probably safer to drive at night where, unless there is someone coming without lights you could see a car through the trees for perhaps a hundred yards, even round the bends. The hills had been logged off some years previously and had not been reseeded. Old stumps stood up amongst the ocean of green new growth stretching as far as you could see. The road was cut strait into the side of the hill and was overhung with bushes bent down with dust thrown up from the road.

Up the 3000 my father drove, as slowly as possible in second gear, trying to conserve the car's suspension. For quite a long time all went well. Then, as we were climbing round a bend, a car coming the other way suddenly appeared. We were spared from a collision by some inches and looked ahead. All you could see was a solid wall of dust, which poured into the car before the windows could be hastily wound up.

Both the occupants and the upholstery were instantly covered with a layer of fine dirt and an application of the windshield wipers merely smeared the stuff around. We crept on at some 5 miles an hour instead of ten! We decided to pull off the road as far as possible and have lunch.

It took us over two hours to reach the valley floor on the other side of the mountain. I don't know what my parents thought about the place, it must have looked a bit desolate to them, but they were not the kind of people to throw out their opinions lightly. As for me, I remember feeling decidedly uncertain.

Valsetz was a mill town owned by the Valsetz Lumber Company. Free enterprise consisted of one privately run store (as I remember) and a church that was lying in a derelict half finished state on the right of the road as you entered the town. I was told later that the minister had become rather disillusioned!

Fresh food was supplied by the company ranch further up the valley.

The food was the reason why men would come to work at Valsetz. All the single men ate in a long mess-hall which was divided into two parts, with a door at each end. The end nearer the mill was for the millworkers, or sliver-pickers, and the other end for the loggers, or men. I was to become a sliver-picker. The food, which consisted of ham and eggs and hotcakes for breakfast, steak for lunch and steak for dinner, was served by waitresses, the most impressive of whom was "Tiny," just over seven feet tall!

On entering the town we enquired the way to Mr. Brownjohn, and were directed to a house with a well-kept garden and lawn across on the other side of a railroad track. With some hesitation I walked up the grey wooden steps on to the verandah and knocked on the door (a small sign on the lawn said "Superintendent's Office"). The door was opened by a middle aged woman in an apron and I asked for the superintendent. In a few minutes Brownjohn came out from the dark interior of the house and to my surprise he was not an Indian at all. He had a gruff voice and was heavy set.

He asked me what I wanted and I handed him the letter. He said O.K., I was hired and was to start work on Monday, the next day, with the Bull Gang run by Stan Henry, at $1.73 an hour.

Then he just turned his back on me, went in and closed the door. I don't remember saying that I accepted and I think it was taken for granted that if there was a job for me I would take it. I may have had the time and courage to thank him. Two things were clear, the pay was good and I hadn't the slightest idea what a Bull Gang was. Regarding the pay, it compared very well with that of my father, an engineer in Portland who earned $80 for a 40 hour week. In 1951 the U.S. minimum wage was $0.75 an hour. (Incidentally silver dollars were still in normal circulation and gold was $32 an ounce!) I went back with the good news to my parents, took my case from the trunk and watched them drive off, leaving me to my fate.

I had been told that there was a group of bunkhouses for the single men. I went over to a group of millhands standing in front of the dancehall, trying to look as old as possible and feeling very young. They looked me over with no sign of interest and I asked one of them, one not too old and not too young, how I could go about getting a bunk in one of the bunkhouses. From the dusty road he led me along a wooden trestle walkway out along over the marshy grass by the edge of the lake. We found a slight and stooping husk of a man in very faded blue jeans and shirt, who looked after the bunkhouses. He told me that I could have a bunk for $1.75 a week and that meals in the mess hall were $0.75 each.

I was out to save money and I thought that I could get by on less than $0.75 a meal, but decided that since the job might be hard I had better get three good meals a day. So I told him I'd take the lot and he led me along further boardwalks past rows of small frame huts that were individual bunkhouses built to hold four men each. I was to move in with Old George, Young George and Blackie.

Each cabin was built up on pilings and had a little verandah, on which was stocked a pile offcuts from the mill, a chopping block and a single bitted axe. On the left on entering was a small cast iron stove. Four paces across under the rather dirty window were piled two stacks of beer cases, one about four feet high and the other stacked to the ceiling. No liquor or beer was sold in the town and it all had to be brought in from Falls City (for the beer), or all the way from Dallas if it was whiskey. There was no State Liquor Store any nearer.

At each end of the bunkhouse, on the right and on the left, were two beds, each with two grey blankets and to my surprise, sheets. Above each bed was a cupboard and at the end, under another small window, a small table. There were also two chairs, and an electric light. My bunk was to be the one on the far side to the left, across from Blackie. The two Georges occupied the other end.

It was Sunday afternoon. Only Blackie was there, and although I don't remember, his first reaction on meeting me must have been to offer me a beer. He too must have taken me down to the mess hall for my first meal.

Meals were simple but substantial. Potatoes, vegetable and as many huge steaks as you could wish, each about three quarters of an inch thick and nine inches long! There were large amounts of coffee and milk, and fruit pies for dessert. As you went out there was a large box of toothpicks tacked to the wall. For this sort of food it was worth working at Valsetz so far from the nearest Liquor store.

Blackie was a small man with, somewhat obviously, jet black hair. He was very proud of the age of his blue jeans (!) and had previously been a window washer of San Francisco skyscrapers. He said that he had become so good at it that he had started to become careless, not a good thing in such an occupation. Although small with a roundish face he was very wiry and had lots of stamina. He worked on the log pond selecting logs and bringing them into the mill, as well as on the "re-load" on the far side of the pond where smaller pulp logs were loaded onto railroad cars to be taken down the Valley & Siletz Railroad to Independence, and then on down the Willamette River to the paper mills.

He was surprised to find out that I was English and he later confided that during the war he had served with the British 8th Army in North Africa and had also been an anti-aircraft gunner for some time in Malta, with a ration, quickly used up, of only four shells a day! How it was that he was with the British rather than the U.S. military I never found out.

Later that Sunday evening Young and Old George came in. Young George must have been like many millworkers, not particularly strong but strong enough, rather slender and well on the way to be physically worn out. He was probably in his late thirties, and his hair was receding, (so was his chin!) He was always affable but slightly seedy. Single, he was attracted to girls. He had a small printed sign hanging from the rear view mirror in his 1937 Plymouth "Tickle my Billie and I'll tickle your Nellie," but I never saw a girl in the car with him. I think that he spent most of his pay on drinks and women each weekend, partly in the saloon at Falls city and partly further off, perhaps as far as Portland. He worked somewhere up by the head-rig, deep in the heart of the mill.

Old George was in his seventies. He had worked on steam threshing machines on the prairies in Canada in the 1890's. He used to spend much of his time in the bunkhouse listening to the radio and he returned home every weekend to Silverton on the other side of Salem. As I would usually try to hitch-hike up to Portland in the weekend he would sometimes take me as far as Salem on a Friday night. Perhaps he worked somewhere in the planing mill, because I never remember seeing him during working hours and I was never curious enough to ask him what he did. It had to be a light job though, at least by lumber mill standards. One little oddity of his was that he considered it dangerous to drive a car at night with the lights on high-beam, so we would drive for miles along the empty highway with them dipped!

Early in the morning the mill whistle would blow and we would get up. At first I found that my feet were ice cold and that I had slept badly. This was because the blankets were either made for a relatively small man or, more likely, had shrunk following many washings, and I am over six feet tall. The temperatures in daytime were often in the high nineties, sometimes over a hundred, but at night they would drop considerably. In my sleep I would pull the blankets up round my neck and leave my feet sticking out. Then I would have to draw my legs up under me to try to get them warm. This made my knees poke out as neither the bunk nor the blankets were very wide. This made Blackie roar with laughter.

After a couple of nights of fitful sleeping I took the two blankets and made a complicated labyrinth seal between them. As long as I didn't move too much the seal would last until morning. If not, cold air would come in round my stomach, in which case drawing up my legs didn't help at all, and I had to fumble with my fingers for a cure.

It wasn't generally worthwhile lighting the stove in the morning, as we only had time to eat and go to work. If the morning was chilly Blackie would take a little whiskey, stored in the cupboard above his head, before breakfast. If not, perhaps a couple of beers. Sometimes Old George would go out and chop some firewood and light the stove.

The first time I tried to take a turn at chopping wood he was amazed to see that I was almost completely incompetent. He could hardly believe that I had passed right through childhood without having to chop wood, even in the suburbs of London. Every clever method that I had learnt as a Sea Scout seemed to be forgotten as he watched me either try to sever the fingers on my left hand or beat the wood to a pulp. My efforts to split this firewood provided comic entertainment for the others. It certainly didn't improve my aim to have a small but critical audience of mill workers looking on. Just as I was about to bring down the axe I'd hear, "He's gonna miss!"

"Damn you, I'm not!" I said to myself, but of course he was right.

Before I could start work I had to report to the Company doctor, who had his office in the railroad station. Passenger trains no longer came up to Valsetz although the U.S. Mail was still delivered by a "speeder" which occasionally carried passengers. I regret that I never took the ride down to Independence.

I thought that I'd just have a routine check. All was fine until, after the examination, he started to fill out forms. "Where do you live?"

"Portland, Oregon."

"Name of parents?"

"Herbert Collard and Marjorie Collard."

"Date of birth?"

"6 September-er-1931."

Quite clever, I thought, by saying I'm nineteen he's not liable to think that I'm only seventeen.

"Draft Card?"

Of course I didn't have one, and I thought I'd have to say I'd lost it. Luckily, stress brought inspiration, "Being English I don't have to have one," I replied. The doctor didn't seem to be convinced, but said he'd check on it. I left his office wondering what would happen when he found out that all adult male immigrants had to register with the Draft Board. Luckily for me, nothing ever became of it.

Monday morning I went along to the mill with the other mill workers and stood around where I was told Stan Henry would appear. What would he be like?

He turned out to be over seventy years old. His hair was thick, curly, completely white and more or less hidden under a strange red conical shaped hat. All men in the woods wear either red or yellow headgear. Stan Henry's hat was an old felt logger's one which had the brim pulled down so many times that it had been transformed into an extension of the crown. He wore heavy denim trousers held up by suspenders. Caulk boots, with the caulks worn off, laced up high, and a faded flannel shirt. I never saw him dressed in any other rig.

Some years previously the men had given him a curly pipe with a silver lid, in which he smoked "Peerless" tobacco. When not smoking (by the mill it was quite obviously forbidden) he chewed the "Peerless," the yellow packet of which he kept in one of his shirt front pockets. In the other he had, apparently, small sticks of dynamite! He turned out to be an ideal boss for the Bull Gang. Other activities seemed to take up much of his time so we weren't pushed too hard on the job. He told me that he had worked on the building of the mill in 1919. Despite his age he was still as strong as any two of the men working for him.

Stan Henry with a peavey

The Bull Gang was supposed to do all the odd jobs round the mill and in the town of Valsetz, and was made up of the old and feeble, the slackers and the young and incompetent. I met the requirements in the last category. I quickly became pretty good at shoveling, despite the multitude of blisters it raised on my hands.

For the first week I got up every morning feeling as though my back was about to break and my hands on fire. It seemed that the thing was to be a boss, but that I needed a bit more practice before I could apply for the position.

A few weeks before I arrived the Polk County Health Department had visited Valsetz. The Valsetz Lumber Company was told that unless sewage removal conditions were improved the town would be closed. This improvement was going to be carried out by the Bull Gang, so the County's action was, indirectly, the reason why I had been hired.

The first modifications had, it appeared gone with a bang. The week before I started work it was decided that drainage from the marsh would be much improved if a sort of canal could be dug from near some sheds, (where planed lumber was loaded into box cars), across parallel to the bunkhouses and so to the lake. This way lay by the end of the bunkhouses where there was the block with toilets and showers. Since these were not drained the job of digging the canal was going to be, to say the least, indelicate. Stan Henry, so I was told, took pity on his gang and decided to blast the whole drainage ditch with dynamite.

He set about it in such a way that the contents would be blown up leaving a ditch with bare vertical sides, so that later "tidying up" would be kept to a minimum. He planted his explosives along the route to be taken and led the wires back to the mill office, nearer to the mill and also on pilings. Brownjohn himself came to preside at the event. The plunger was pressed and a wall of stinking mud rose high in the air, leaving a very well "blown" ditch. Stan Henry was about to be congratulated when a sudden strong gust of wind blew the ditches contents over the rows of bunkhouses.

For the next few days the Bull Gang was engaged in hosing down the bunkhouses in such a way, that if Stan Henry was standing on one side of a cabin he was pretty sure to receive a dose of water coming from the other side!

I arrived just in time for the rebuilding of the municipal sewer lines. The central part of the town had what could roughly be called main drainage, the parts further out relying on septic tanks. The Bull Gang was told to rip the old lines, made of four wooden boards nailed together, enlarge the trench and relay concrete pipe about thirty inches diameter. As the lines passed more often than not directly under the houses the working space was very cramped. Kneeling down in the bottom of the ditch in the "water" one could just squeeze underneath. The newcomer, immediately christened either "English" or "Slim" was sent in first with a pick. The debris removed, being the remains of the wooden drain and its contents, was shoveled to the rear and out from under the house by others. This was perhaps the only time that the "slackers" worked as hard as the rest. Had they not they would have been buried, and not only that, the occupants in the houses continued to use their toilets despite (or perhaps to enjoy) our loud complaints! It was interesting to note that Brownjohn's brother was one of the slackers, he was ordered to go in just behind me, and I was told to work as fast as I could! The result was dismay for the brother and joy for the rest of the Gang.

The ground at Valsetz was full of rocks, so digging the trenches for the new sewage system took some effort. A team of two men was supposed to dig 30 feet a day. Every morning we went over to the mill's forge to collect newly sharpened picks for the day. The two men worked on the "I'll pick and you shovel" system and by spelling each other and not stopping 30 feet was (just) possible. Work could be held up though, when we came across an exceptionally large boulder, greater than a standard "one-man" or "two-man" one.

It was during this job that I first became of a sense of physical competition that exists in places like Valsetz. There was a man called Peterson, always neatly dressed, who drove a truck and who had the monopoly on garbage collecting in the town. It was he who delivered the concrete pipe. As his truck moved slowly forward two of us would lift a pipe from off the truck and lay it on the roadside. These pipes were heavy and it wasn't easy to lay them down gently, so they wouldn't get nicked. Peterson came back to give us a hand, proceeding to help by taking of the concrete pipes alone. He didn't even have to help, since he was the owner of the truck. He was much stronger than any of us and just wished to let us know.

A few days after this they were short handed in the mill. Jobs there are either very specialized and require considerable skill or they are easy in every way except hard work. I was sent to make my start on one of these easier jobs, the green chain.

The logs are brought in by logging trucks from the woods, these trucks being "off-the road" types that were too big to be allowed on the public highway, but could carry enormous amounts of timber. In the cool of the evening you could hear drivers getting in a final load before nightfall; as they came down off the mountain with a far off bellowing of engines in low gear. While we sat on the steps of the bunkhouse drinking stubby after stubby of beer they were still at work.

This beer was provided under an unusually generous arrangement. Neither Blackie, or Old or Young George had had too much schooling, and they were most impressed by the fact that I was at university. They were even more impressed by the cost of going, and thought that it was obvious that if I was going to earn my fees for the following year in just one summer I wouldn't have any spare cash to spend on beer. They therefore ordered me to drink with them at all times and to pay nothing towards the cost. There was little that I could do to repay such generosity. As far as Young George could see, the only positive thing about university was that there were plenty of young girls freely available!

When the logging trucks arrived they dumped their loads in the lake. The logs were then sorted and according to the mill's orders brought in rafts to the log pond. Blackie would stand apparently motionless on the raft pushing with all his might against the railroad bridge. Then, very slowly he would take a step forward, then another. Out on the logs in the afternoon sun it must have been exhausting. After four or five minutes he could stop, and the logs would glide very, very slowly towards the mill. One man could move a small raft by pushing hard long enough. Sometimes he would use a small winch on the bank at the entrance to the mill, which was incredibly low geared. All you had to do was turn the crank a few hundred times and the logs would come in at the end of a long steel cable.

One at a time the logs were pushed into the dock below the head rig. Two chains were attached to beams on one side of the dock, hanging down to the bottom of the dock and then coming up the other side to the log deck high above the water. Steam windlasses wound in the cable and the log was hauled up until it rolled out onto the log deck. The chains were then slackened off and lowered back down into the dock ready for the next log. There was no let up.

Work was carried out as fast as possible. The mill cut 150,000 board feet a day, most of which was dried in the kilns, planed and then loaded into boxcars to be shipped "back East."

The Head Rig

15

Everything of any size in Valsetz was powered by steam. As the windlasses tightened the chain plumes of white steam would shoot out of the side of the building and the log would slowly come free from the pond, with bits of bark and water streaming off its sides and back down into the water. From the bank (where I would sometimes go during my "smoke break") you could see men above rolling the logs over using peaveys with cant hooks. It was not a job for beginners.

The logs were then carried on chain tracks to the side of the head rig itself. This rig is a very large vertical bandsaw with teeth on both sides of the blade. Set in the floor is what amounts to a short piece of railroad track. Between the tracks is a cable having a loop around a drum at each end of the track.

On the track rides a carriage, and on the carriage is the log. The driver of the carriage, who rides on it with the log, is the head sawyer, whose job was considered to be the most important one in the mill. From his seat on the carriage he can survey the log and decide just how it should be cut for maximum profit. He pulls a lever and steam jacks toss the log, up to about five feet in diameter, onto the carriage. Then, using smaller jacks and chain tracks on the carriage itself the sawyer turns and lines up log for the first cut. The carriage then runs the log through the saw and jacks flip it so that all the following cuts are made with the log on a flat base. The carriage then proceeds back and forth with the log being progressively turned into the most profitable of timbers.

The head sawyer made about four dollars an hour in 1951 and earned every penny of it. On his judgment of the best ways of cutting each log rested the profit or loss of the company. I was told that every fall the head sawyer at Valsetz went hunting, and the mill was closed while he was gone.

After the head rig the timbers passed through edgers and trimmers, became boards, and then passed as green timber down to a big "table" to be sorted. This was the green chain, of which I had been warned before going to Valsetz. As each board arrives onto the chain tracks running along the table it is marked so that it can be pulled off and stacked neatly in piles, four feet wide, on wooden blocks.

The quality of the wood coming through the mill was very high, from "select" (close straight grained boards with no knots), "number 1" (straight grained with small knots allowed), "number 2" (probably wider grained and with bigger knots). The rest was "number 8," not worth wasting time on. This last went the full length of the chain and fell off at the end in a pile. What happened to it afterwards I don't remember. Most of the wood was either Douglas Fir or Hemlock, but occasionally there would be Cedar, which gave a lovely smell. Once we had some pinkish coloured stuff, apparently sound wood that made the whole mill smell like a gin factory!

The sun seems to strike particularly fiercely on the green chain, and I quickly found out that I sweated far too much to wear my glasses. I worked in the constant hope that a machine up the line, or the chain itself would break down. On a nearby pillar a small salt tablet dispenser had been nailed. These tablets made up for the loss of strength due to sweating, and you took one only when it seemed absolutely necessary. The drinking of water was just not on, as it only made you sweat more. The body's liquid level was restored to normal after work by drinking large quantities of beer in the evening.

Besides the marker, an older man of experience, there are some five or six men down the chain. Each has several piles to fill. It was on the green chain that I found out why steel capped boots were required by law. To receive the end of a railroad tie on the end of an ordinary leather boot would be more than just painful! Mine cost thirteen dollars, were supposed to withstand half a ton dropped from some great height, and certainly saved my ten toes. They lost their shine in about two hours on the green chain.

The younger men stripped to the waist in the heat of the day, when the temperature reached 104°F in the shade. Older men kept their wool shirts and undershirts on. We all wore heavy duty gloves and big leather aprons. All morning we would have boards up to three deep coming down, nonstop. This was sometimes made worse by railroad ties coming along with the boards, with them, but by some strange law of nature, usually on top of them! For some reason the ties went further down the chain and piles of one by fours had to be pulled out from under them and stacked before rushing off to drag off the tie. The greatest crime was to stop the chain.

The man on my left, further up the chain was a Southerner named Paul (pronounced Pau'), from whom I picked up a bit of a Louisiana accent to add to my London one. He would come and help me if I became completely overwhelmed. After lunch we would start the chain before the whistle blew to get the chain clear and have a head start. It gave us great pleasure to be able to stand idle, waiting for the first boards to arrive, and watching everyone else working away in the distance.

I forget if it was Paul or someone else working in the same place who didn't turn up one Monday morning. For a man to do this was accepted from time to time, as he could have been dead drunk only a few hours before and hadn't sobered up enough to get to work before the whistle blew. Something must have happened as he didn't arrive all morning and he was roundly cursed by every one of us on the chain, working shorthanded. Even the marker had to help to pull boards.

He still hadn't arrived by lunchtime and we had to start again in the afternoon without him. Even though we cleared off the chain before the whistle "blewed" we soon got behind again.

At two o'clock he arrived, looking in a bad way and as if he still had not recovered from the night before. Nothing more than a few "goddamns" were said but he knew that he had been cursed all the morning. For perhaps a quarter of an hour he pulled lumber beside me before I woke up to the fact that he was pulling with only one arm!

It turned out that the night before he had had too much to drink and had driven his car off the road on the way in from Falls City. This in itself was not particularly unusual, as it happened about once a week on average during the summer that I was at Valsetz. Unfortunately for him he had been trapped underneath his car, jammed against a stump, until about mid-morning. Luckily he was then seen waving by the driver of a truck who was on his way in. Nobody else had seen the new wreck down off the road.

The next day he seemed alright again, in his faded work clothes and leather apron.

Railroad ties, about eight feet long, are very heavy and their short length was bad news for the man who had to pull them. Apparently they were for a narrow gauge railroad as otherwise, although being heavier, they would have been easier to handle. The problem was that they could not be slid over the rollers on the edge of the chain directly onto the pile, but had to be lifted and carried for a short distance between the two. With railroad ties a stack is quickly made so you are forever leaping down to set blocks for a new stack, immediately the straddle carrier took the completed one away, and then up again to pull more ties.

When you pull the first tie on a pile you have to jump down with it. You have to do the same with the following ones until the first layer is complete, and from then on you can slide them.

With a long board you can just about reach the far block without leaving the walk way, and after the first one is place you can slide the next one out along on top of the first one. You lean towards the chain, grab the board with both hands and throw your weight back with a jerk. The board is thus snatched and slides forward off the chain. As it reaches the point where it just balances on the roller you can swing it so that it points at the place on the stack where it should go. The end falls neatly half on and half off the board next to its place and slides out across the incomplete stack. At the last moment a quick twist makes the far end fall in place next to the one it was riding on. Then with one hand you flip the near end and the board falls right in place.

This, of course, does not happen on your first day on the job. The chain seemed to me to be moving twice as fast as it really did. I rushed madly from bay to bay and from stack to stack. The boards had to be stacked very neatly so that the straddle carrier could be driven in to pick them up. It was then that I sweated so much I could no longer see out through my glasses. By noon I felt that I couldn't possibly finish the day. Money and pride are, however, powerful incentives and of course I went back after lunch. After all, a little work shouldn't get a full grown man of "nineteen" down!

Just after starting on the green chain I received a powerful aid in the form of Homer Ames. He was a Northwest Indian, and I found him working next to me. When it seemed that I must stop the chain, with boards being up to six feet "downstream" from their piles he would suddenly appear as if by magic, stacking boards for me at incredible speed and seemingly without effort. He rarely spoke and moved in complete silence, although he wore heavy boots like the rest of us. He never seemed to hurry but he worked very fast. I remember that the rake of his nose was at about the same angle as the crown of his work hat. He was the only Indian that I met at Valsetz, and I only wish that I'd known him better.

A Miller Straddle Carrier

In overhauling the mill it had been decided that there was about ten years of lumber left out in the woods. Neither the timber decking around the mill nor the drying kilns for the lumber would last that long. The whole mill was built on piling, except of course, the power station, and inside millwrights, both those of the Valsetz Lumber Company and of a contracting company were at work rebuilding what was necessary. They were also installing a chipper to chip up waste wood for pulp. A short railroad spur would have to be run in to the chipper to receive its output.

The timber decking on which lumber was stacked and the straddle carriers drove was to be replaced by a gravel fill. This job was to be done by Stan Henry and his bull gang, aided by two bulldozers and a truck (instead of dynamite!) One of the first things I was told to do was to chop off the ends of some big beams, two feet square that protruded across a ditch that we'd dug. This wasn't easy as I had to be down in the ditch to do it and there wasn't much room. Stan Henry must have known that I was useless with an axe when he gave me the job. He told me that he wanted it dressed off absolutely smooth. It was a Friday and at the end of the day I was still chipping away. Stan Henry told me that it was a good way for me to learn how to use a double bitted axe. The next day we all worked overtime and I managed to finish to his satisfaction. I have the feeling that he found pleasure in teaching real life to this young, callow foreigner.

One of the others working overtime had an Oldsmobile, reasonably new, perhaps 1948. The Friday we had been paid and he had been to Dallas for the evening. On the way back he had side-swiped another car but had kept on going. He was in his twenties and had the reputation of being "independent." Saturday a Polk County Deputy Sheriff arrive in Valsetz along with the man who had been side-swiped.

The following I only saw from a distance, as I was told that I should keep away.

It appears that the Deputy asked for the Valsetz owner of the Oldsmobile, and was told that he was working. So he went over to discuss the matter with the guilty one, who denied all knowledge of the incident. The Deputy then suggested that he would like to look at the car, and we all trailed over to see the outcome. It was then that I was told, in no uncertain terms, to keep well away. The Oldsmobile was parked in the area in front of the dancehall. It was bent and apparently had paint from the other car on it. The Valsetz millworker said it was just a coincidence, and the Deputy replied that he was going to "take him in." The Valsetz man said he wouldn't go.

Slim watched breathlessly from a safe distance, over by some loading sheds. In the hot sun the Deputy fidgeted with his uniform. The fellow with him, whose car had been hit looked even hotter and uncomfortable. He too was probably from a mill. The Deputy said something about taking him in whether he wanted to go or not.

It was then that I noticed that not everyone in the crowd that had formed had laid down his tool, which would normally be the case for the slightest reason. A number still held axes, peaveys and other "heavy" tools. The Deputy looked at the crowd, looked more ill at ease, but after a moment said he would have to take him in, by force if necessary. Then a voice from the crowd told the Deputy to, "Get out of Valsetz!" After a moment's reflection the officer swore and said okay, he would leave, but he would lie in wait to catch the culprit on the other side of Falls City.

Since there was no other way out of Valsetz, except by the railroad, it seemed a pretty sure thing. The two men left town but I never heard of the Valsetz man being arrested.

It was at Valsetz that I learnt to drive a truck. Most of the decking around the mill had been cut through, and had been dragged away by a D-8 Caterpillar to be burnt at a safe distance from the mill itself. Most of the uprights supporting the decking had been built up resting on piles of cedar blocks, pit blocks, lying deep in the ooze underneath. The mill had been built in 1919, but none of these blocks were in the slightest way rotten. They were about 12 x 24s, four feet long, completely water soaked. Stan Henry's bull gang was to go down and dig them out so that they could be recuperated for further use.

Under the sun, over a hundred in the shade, the ooze dried out rapidly enough to get a truck in. For use around the mill there were two trucks, both army surplus. One was a Dodge used by the millwrights and the other a G.M. or Chevrolet four wheel drive dump truck. For some reason, perhaps it was the weekend, there was no driver available.

"Any of you guys know how to drive a truck?" asked Stan Henry.

It didn't take me very long to compare driving the truck with floundering in the ooze wrestling with soggy, foul smelling pit blocks. So, somewhat to my own surprise I heard myself saying that I did! In fact I had only had very limited experience driving my father's Dodge, first under parental supervision (to learn enough to get my driver's license), and then from time to time on my own.

"O.K. English, take the truck and go and get the tools," said Stan.

I climbed up into the cab, where I had never been before, and groped around. Army trucks are built to be driven by amateurs, and luckily there was a metal plaque riveted to the dashboard showing the gearshift arrangement. There was two other levers between the seats, one for selecting four wheel drive and the other for raising the bed. I had no idea which was which. Furthermore I had never driven any kind of vehicle with a floor gear shift and it also took me quite a time to find the starter. At last I found it, pushed it to the floor and waited for the explosion. The engine caught right away and off I roared in low gear and, taking an eternity between gear changes, finally making it into top.

I probably shouldn't have worried about my lack of ability though, as I may well have been no worse a truck driver than any of the others. It was unlikely that any of them had had any experience with a truck so I wasn't really any worse off than them. The important thing was that I had been the first to speak up!

Stan Henry could drive and he had a brand new Chevy with "Powerglide" automatic transmission. It could be that fluid drive had been invented expressly for him as he seemed to have no idea regarding coordination between the clutch and the accelerator. During working hours he drove a thirty-six or seven Dodge, cut down to make it a pickup. On this machine he would drive around town, often with as many members of the bull gang as could pile on riding on the homemade pickup bed. To slow down Stan Henry used only one item; he pushed in the clutch, leaving his foot down on the accelerator! It was easy to know when he wanted to slow down just listening to the sudden howl of the engine.

Coming round the planing shed we had the occasional exciting duel with a straddle carrier coming at us. It could be at high speed, fully loaded and being driven backwards. There was never any collision as straddle carrier drivers were very skilled and could take evasive action, and they were probably well aware of Stan Henry's driving skills. For them there was, of course, no question of braking with a full load of newly planed planks underneath. I remember thinking that if the carrier was empty there was possibly just enough room for us to go between its legs.

The back of the "pickup" was built up of boards bolted to the chassis, being just a flat bed without sides. On this all the axes, saws, shovels, picks and peaveys would be loaded and everyone would climb on. The car had had a hard life, its springs were tired and of course not suitable for taking a "pickup load." This load was the weight of all the members of the bull gang who would climb on and sit with their legs dangling over the edge of the platform. As we started off the tires would rub against the bed and after a couple of blocks or so smoke would be pouring up. As Valsetz wasn't a very big place and we didn't go very far fire never took hold.

As time went by I became more proficient at driving the dump truck. At first I allowed it to get overloaded in the ooze and got stuck, having then to call in the aid of the small bulldozer to push me out. Once he too, in trying to help me, got stuck as well and we had to ignominiously wait for the big D.8 to come over and give us both a shove. I liked driving the truck as it was easier work. The rest of the bull gang didn't seem to mind the set-up as each time I became stuck they had an excuse to stop work. Stan Henry never said anything either, although he saw what was happening. Brownjohn would not have approved had he known. Perhaps he did but I think that he would have hesitated giving orders to a man who was so much senior to him, and who had taken part in the mill's actual construction. Stan Henry was obviously someone special!

One day I was sent alone with the truck to get some big barrels of paint from the railroad car and take them over to some sheds near the dry kilns. I drove down to the siding where the Valley & Siletz Railroad's only boxcar lay in state. It was an old wooden one with both diamond framed trucks and truss rods underneath. Although it was in daily use on the Valley & Siletz it was no longer allowed out on the Southern Pacific's line. Looking at it made me wonder how many hoboes had actually "ridden its rods." The weather beaten boxcar brown paint had turned to powder, but it was still just possible to make out the faded letters "Valley & Siletz." As I remember its number was 23. Rolling back the door I could see several steel drums inside. Each of them had had the weight of its contents stenciled on the outside: 400 lbs. wt.. Even without the contents the drums themselves were hardly light weight. However it wasn't too difficult getting them out as the truck bed was about an inch lower than the sill of the boxcar and I could roll them out on their rims.

When I got to where I was to unload them I was presented with the very real problem of how to unload them. I wasn't at all sure what to do but I went off and found some heavy 4 x 12s, of which I selected the two, longest ones. These I carried back to the truck and propped them up against the back. I aimed both truck and props so that the drums, in rolling down the incline would have the longest run possible to slow down.

I made sure the props were really secure, turned the first barrel over on its side (no easy job), and rolled it to the top of the incline. The stage was set and I pushed on it very slowly.

The barrel immediately took charge, roared off down my "ramp," careened across the shed's floor and smashed into a pile of boards that I had tried to avoid! Why it didn't burst open I don't know. The steel barrels themselves must have been extremely strong.

Hearing the immense crash brought Otto, who was working nearby, over to see if I needed any help. This he did, but first a few words about him.

If you are of normal size look down at your ankle. It will be noticeably smaller than Otto's wrist. He was the boss of a group of millwrights contracted to rebuild the drying kilns, and I sat next to him in the mess-hall. We always had the same place at table. His appetite was huge and he was quite able to devour three very big steaks at a sitting. On finishing one he would make the comment "I'll just have another small sample," reach across the table, take the platter, slide another steak onto his plate and wade in. This washed down by mugs of coffee and would be finished off with several helpings of apple and peach pie. I must add that he was most friendly and often used to drive me up to Portland on a Friday evening.

The first barrel had rolled with such force across the shed I was scared to let another one go unguided. It was obvious though that to steady the barrel on the planks leading down from the truck was not a good idea, as you could easily get crushed by it if it got away. While wondering what I was going to do I kept on moving the remaining barrels from the front to the back of the truck.

Otto's arrival with an offer to help was thus more than welcome. He was so strong that he could no doubt steady the barrel on its way down. He was a much better judge of the situation than I, and if it did get out of hand it wouldn't be me underneath it. He asked me as my back was turned getting another barrel, "Hey, English, want some help?" I answered yes and went on heaving on my barrel. When I had got it to the back of the truck I turned round.

To my astonishment, there was Otto with his arms wrapped around one of the drums, slowly waddling away with it across the shed floor! His eyes were popping under the strain and the color of his straight fair hair stood out in strong contrast against his bright red face. One by one he carried each of those four hundred pound barrels off the bed of the truck and put them down about twenty feet away. It was an amazing feat of strength. It put my puny efforts at getting the timbers and making my ramp into perspective.

On Friday evenings Otto left Valsetz for Portland. He had a long chassis Chevy pickup about a year old. It was painted green and belonged to his company, the Associated Wood Products, and it had a metal frame fixed on the back so that it could be used for carrying long boards or poles. He wasn't one to waste time and left Valsetz five minutes after quitting time. If there was no work on Saturday I went with him—if I could get ready in five minutes. It paid to get away as fast as possible as every Friday a long stream of cars left town, although not many went as far as Portland.

The idea was to drive out without being overtaken, and the record for the time to do the seventeen miles to Falls City was just under half an hour. This was really good going considering the state of the road between the two places.

With Otto you were sure to be one of the first to leave town. Most men stayed a while to get spruced up before going out for their week-end "on the town." Otto drove with one hand on the spokes of the steering wheel and his foot hard down. In fact he steered with his left hand so that his right one could hold a "stubby." A bag with half a dozen of these small bottles of beer was wedged between the two front seats of the pickup. With my mind focused on trying to earn as much money as possible in the summer I remember being aghast when he idly tossed the empties out the window. There was a five cents deposit on each!

Once, on the road to Falls City, as we slid round a blind corner with Otto's foot hard down we met a large car coming the other way. Seeing us at the last moment it shot to the left and hit the bank as we whizzed by.

"Christ! That was Brownjohn," shouted Otto, as we raced round the next bend at high speed.

Otto was in a class by himself, but I did do my best to prevent him from drinking all the beer while driving. I think that it was just after we turned on to Highway 99W at Rickreall that a "pit-stop" for a few more bottles was made. When we arrived in Portland he let me off downtown by the Journal building and would leave me for the weekend. From there I would make my rather unsteady way home by bus (or even by the Council Crest street-car if was still running in 1951).

I have no idea why Otto came up to Portland every Friday. Perhaps he was married and had his home there. Certainly Associated Wood Products had its office there and he may have been obliged to report on the state of the job at Valsetz every Saturday.

Otto's team at Valsetz was, amongst other things, building a new chipper and new dry kilns for drying the wood coming off the green chain. All the ends and offcuts from the lumber, as it was processed, were thrown down through holes in the mill's floor which were over small conveyor chains that lead to one big central one. This main conveyer sloped up right across the mill and then out to the burner. Just as it left the mill building was the "hog" into which most of the scraps were fed and instantly ground up into hog fuel, that fed the mill's, and in fact all the town's power station's boilers. Otto's men and the Valsetz millwrights had led a new conveyor off the main one that led to the chipper. All good scraps, without a trace of bark on them were taken and thrown onto this new belt, taken to the chipper and dumped into large box cars built without any roof. In one week two men made enough chips to fill about eight cars.

The bull gang was given the job of lengthening the railroad spur leading under and past the chipper. This spur was to run alongside the mill between the head rig and the lake. All along the edge of the lake were huge mounds of hog fuel for the power station, and the spur, which would at this point only be used for empty cars, was to be built on a fill of this fuel.

At this time I was working with two "old timers." Now relegated to the bull gang they could still work well enough but both had been crippled some years earlier in the woods. In their fifties, they were still very strong, but whereas one could no longer bend down the other could no longer raise weights above his waist. Working together as a team they were as good as any other two men working independently, although at times they looked rather comical to anyone who didn't know the reason.

Since I had progressed reasonably well in the art of truck driving I was allowed to have a go with a small bulldozer, being used to build the sawdust fill.

A bulldozer is nothing like a truck to drive, I found, especially on a heap of sawdust, but I began to manage it quite well. Peterson, who would normally have driven it, was away elsewhere. I was kept busy pushing sawdust along to the edge of the lake and then into it. Eventually a fill began to appear over which the bulldozer could be driven to extend the fill even further. It made me feel as if I was driving on the top of a huge sponge cake.

In the afternoon my luck ran out. I got the cat too near to the edge and it started to tip. In trying to back out the tracks sunk into the sawdust and the machine tipped further. It was biting out the sponge cake from underneath itself. At this moment everyone started shouting and I switched off. The lakeside end of the bulldozer was nearly down to water level. There was nothing to do but wait for the return of Peterson. I moved away to find a shovel and watch events from a discreet distance, as I knew that Peterson would not be best pleased when he saw what had happened. He wasn't, and judging by his language he was quite angry, but he did manage to winch it back to safety. I was never asked to drive the bulldozer again!

Old Bill's Gang Saw

One of the most fascinating saws in the mill was a gang-saw, run by Bill, one of the old timers. This saw was roughly equivalent to an edger, but whereas the latter has a row of circular saws the gang saw has a row of vertical blades and is a reciprocating saw (rather like a multi-blade hacksaw), powered directly by steam. I think that it was built in Milwaukee, Wisconsin, at about the turn of the century. It was used for cutting large slabs of high grade hemlock into wood for making door jambs and so on, where a perfect finish was required. The slabs were cut at an angle so that if planed with the grain a smooth satin finish would result. The angle of the cut was perhaps thirty degrees so the wood was quite fragile and would probably have broken off in an edger.

Bill was a great prospector, as were many of the older workers who actually lived in Valsetz. For these men there were at least three pastimes, prospecting, making liquor and (believe it or not) digging for Spanish treasure down on one of the Oregon beaches. Bill, then, was a prospector and every weekend he went out in the hills to try to strike something of interest. One day I visited his bunkhouse. It was heaped with samples of which he was proud and which he was sure contained something valuable. The only problem was that it cost a fair bit of money to have assaying done up in Portland. Knowing that I was in college he asked me if I knew anything about chemistry.

Here was a chance to pay back the generosity I had received from everyone at Valsetz. The only thing was that I had always been a failure at chemistry at school in England and that I hadn't even seen a chemistry book since my arrival in the U.S.A. I remembered though, that my father had a book called "Inorganic Chemistry" on a shelf at home and it was obvious that his samples were not "inorganic." So the next weekend I borrowed the book and brought it back to Valsetz.

It was full of tests by "quantitative and qualitative analysis" and so on, but since the selection of acids available to Bill was very limited I was fortunately restricted to doing "qualitative" tests only.

The first thing to do was to look at the samples. They all looked like stones to me but the prospectors knew better. As it turned out the samples were, on the whole of better quality than those found by Federal Government geologists who had pronounced the region to be arid as far as rich minerals were concerned.

Bill had one chunk that was, as I remember, dark grey with shiny flecks in it. Using the index in the back of the book I looked up everything they could think of. I sat at the table by my bunk with a number of interested spectators around behind me. The two Georges seemed doubtfully proud of my display of deep learning. Blackie, on the other hand, was interested professionally as he too was a prospector.

After about half an hour's playing around we left the samples to analyse themselves, pickled in nitric acid. Then a few days later I made my prognostic. The chunk had manganese in it and also a small amount of platinum. The various tests that I had carried out confirmed the grey color of the rock and also the sparkling bits. The appearance of the sample and my analysis led Bill to wrapping it up and sending it to Portland to have a proper quantitative assay carried out.

I had done what I could, but felt very inadequate. The number of chemicals was so very limited and I knew that I knew next to nothing about the subject. The results of the real assay would not be known for some three weeks.

I asked how was it that they were able to find various minerals in the wilds of the Coast Range. The answer was quite simple but seemed to be extraordinary. If you can use a divining rod to find water, why won't it work for minerals? For instance, to find gold, you take a gold ring and stick it down onto the end of the rod and then walk out to look for gold! This at least was Blackie's method.

Coming from college and having all of one year's study of Physics (which I barely passed) I was obviously skeptical of such a non-scientific method, and it must have showed on my face. Blackie said "O.K., if you don't believe it, we'll show you."

Someone went off and cut a willow stick. In the bunkhouse next to my bed it was trimmed down until just the fork was left. Then we cut a small notch on the end with a penknife and put a nickel in it. Holding the two ends of the forks Blackie held it out over a few nickels that had been put on the table. Slowly the wand bent down towards the nickels, although you couldn't see any movement on Blackie's part. I still felt unconvinced, and I think that anyone who has not seen a rod "in action" is not liable to be a believer. Then, Blackie handed the rod over to me!

The divining rod Works!

Maybe, subconsciously I believed in water divining. As I held the rod out, the thick end away from me and gripping the two ends of the forks like handlebars, but with the palms up, it began to turn. I wasn't conscious of its turning but turn it did. Without the nickel it would go down facing anywhere as the bunkhouses were built out over the marsh by the lake and there was water everywhere below us. With the nickel it wouldn't do it except when held over the money over the table. We stood in a group around the "diviner" stubbies in our hands.

The men were very pleased that it also worked for me and one of them, who really had the touch, said he'd like to give a real demonstration. He put the nickel back in and held it over the coins on the table. The point bent down and he clenched his fists up tight to prevent it. For a while the rod stopped, but you could from the veins standing out on the backs of his hands, that he was having to exert a lot of effort to hold it. Suddenly, down it went, and he relaxed his grip. The bark had peeled off under his hands!

To my regret I never saw the excavations down on the Oregon coast being made in the hope of finding Spanish treasure. It appears that a long time ago either one or two galleons from the Philippines were wrecked somewhere on the Oregon coast. This has been verified, and some years later I was introduced to a man who showed me wax that he'd picked up with the stamped seal of the Philippine government still visible. The wreck of a Spanish vessel had apparently taken place in the eighteenth century near the foot of the Neahkanee Mountain. Indian legends tell of a large ship being wrecked there, and of course it was presumed to be carrying treasure. All Spanish galleons carry treasure, almost as a matter of course.

Using the divining rod and a gold ring a group of mill workers from Valsetz had combed the beaches. At one spot, where a treasure may in fact still be lying, the rod went down, and it was here that they had sunk a shaft. Not much was ever said about the operation, but each weekend a group of them went off to work on the excavation. They had apparently managed to get their shaft a good way down, but had got to the point where it had to be pumped out each week before they could start work in it. They never struck the treasure that summer, to both their and my disappointment. There were some vague hints made that some gold coins had been retrieved but as I was never shown one I'm afraid I didn't really believe it.

Three weeks later the Portland assaying office results returned. There was a high content of manganese, traces of platinum and there was theoretically enough silver as a byproduct to pay for the extraction. Bill was overjoyed and on the strength of my analysis I was approached by Stan Henry to go shares with him in a gold mine he was wanting to exploit. Like most mines it had not yet been proven, but held great promise. Not being much of a gambler I'm afraid that I didn't go in with him. $1.73 an hour basic wage and time and a half on Saturdays seemed a better bet than the hope of infinite riches (perhaps) in the future. I obviously don't have enough '49ers blood in me? I couldn't very well ask Stan Henry where the mine was if I wasn't willing to help him, so I never heard anything more of it.

Bill did not have the capital to exploit his find, which would have required a road being driven in for trucks to carry the ore out.

Unless you found gold or uranium in a fairly rich vein there was no way you could win. A millworker from Valsetz would generally be scared of "management" and of being hooked if he brought in backers from outside. Of this he was probably right, but fear of being exploited by rich capitalists prevented him from ever opening a commercial undertaking.

This distrust in "bosses" was quite natural, especially for anyone over about thirty years old. The thoughts of the conditions during the Depression were still in their minds. Many of the men came from the southern states and had memories of their fleeing to the west coast at that time, under terrible conditions.

Although there was a union at Valsetz at that time it was not much in evidence. I was asked to join but there was no closed shop. Nothing more was said and I never did. I feel that if the men were happy with the food they were ninety percent happy. The union was stronger amongst the married men who lived in company houses in the town and who obviously didn't eat as we did. Their main gripe was that they had to pay for any improvements or repairs that they made to their houses and were only reimbursed when they left Valsetz.

When Bill's gang saw was running I was given my first job in the mill, working as off bearer to it. This was a promotion, as "in the mill" ranked higher in general estimation than "green chain." An off bearer's job on any saw is to straighten up the wood after it is cut and to remove any bits of bark or trash wood that could cause a jam. For handling wood in the mill the universal tool is the pickeroon, which is either like a long boathook or a small hand axe with its head replaced by a very sharp pick. In between the chains and rollers in the mill there were numerous holes down which the trash could be thrown. This trash falls down onto chains below and is carried off to be chipped by the new chipper, ground up as hog fuel for the power station, or burnt in the burner.

At Valsetz the logs were cut on the head rig and then passed through the edgers. An edger is a machine having about seven circular saws fitted on a splined shaft. The saws can thus be set at different spacings along the shaft according to the size of the planks required. The edgerman has a pile of wood coming from the head rig on a chain. He raises the chain (or rather steps on a pedal that causes steam jacks to raise it) and the board moves onto rollers in front of the edger. Here it is lined up either against stops, raised by small steam jacks or, for a small edger, by a man. I think that for a large edger there are two fast chains moving in each direction "buried" in the table just ahead of the edger. By raising one set of chains or the other a large slab can be both translated or slewed. Lining up for the cut is a skilled job as the stops can only be used if the board has a straight edge, and certainly the boards coming from the head rig are rough with bark on both sides.

Each circular saw blade is connected to a pair of calipers which allow the edgerman to move them back and forth along the shaft. With the saw setting made and the board or timber lined up he reaches up above his head and pulls on a lever. Powered rollers lift then shoot up to run the board through the edger. The lever is above his head so that his arms are out of the way when the rollers are raised. The heaviest timber goes through very fast and it wouldn't do to get your hand in the way.

When the boards come off the edgers they came onto a large table and moved slowly down towards the greenchain. All the debris of waste wood and bark had of course been removed by an off bearer. A man sitting in a sort of sunken well decided which boards should go back to be resawn. These were shot off along a conveyer back into the mill to a vertical bandsaw. They then came back onto the table just "upstream" of where the cut slabs from Bill's gang saw came crashing onto the table.

I stood with my long pickeroon on the table straightening up the boards as they came by moving them so that they were only one deep. I also had to take out any knots and bits of bark or broken wood from in between the tracks, otherwise the boards would hang up and start twisting round. The job seemed to be quite an easy one, as long as you got rid of the scraps right away. The knack of spearing the odd bits and then throwing them accurately into one of the holes was quickly acquired. In the hot sun I could get a nice tan, working stripped to the waist.

Bill's saw could cut three slabs at a time and while working on the table you could watch this pile of boards in the process of being cut slowly advancing towards you. With a heavy "thump, thump" of the gang saw the deluge got nearer and nearer, and then with a mighty crash (as it came clear of the saw) up to about a hundred pieces fell on top on the other wood passing on the table. All of a sudden stuff was flying in all directions at all angles. Short pieces from the edges of the slabs fell between the chains and everything started to slew round. The weight of the boards made them ride up over the short pieces which then had to be dug out from underneath a pile of crisscrossed stuff up to four or five boards deep.

Sometimes it was necessary to stop the chain despite all my efforts to get things straightened out. Then to my deep shame, two or three men, making either sarcastic comments or even worse, saying nothing, would come up onto the table to help. They were so much more skillful with a pickeroon than I that I just got in the way. After a few days I learnt to drag boards to each side before the avalanche and to get rid of all the short pieces immediately they fell. There is nothing worse than to bend over the point of the pickeroon against the steel plating between the chains, in a badly aimed stab at the block that is causing all the trouble, especially when performing in front of experienced millworkers. At least you were alone on the hog.

One day I was at work on the greenchain when the mill boss arrived with another fellow beside him. "Come along with us," was all he said, and for some strange reason I wondered, as we climbed up through the mill, if it was to work on the hog.

Imagine a large metal cone some six feet high, standing point upwards on a spindle inside a cylinder. Set around the outside of the cone are rows and rows of sharp knives. The cone is rotated by a one hundred horsepower motor at high speed, so that anything that falls into it is ground up in a flash into "hog fuel" for the boilers of the generating station. This machine, the hog, merits its name since even big chunks of wood falling onto it are ground up immediately with a literally deafening rasping noise.

We walked round the mill and went in a door under the floor of the log deck. Huge wooden beams ran every direction, all painted in a flaking white "fireproof" paint. The whole place reeked of oil and wet wood, and even more so of steam. Above the continuous rumbling of the electric motors that were driving the chains there was a loud hissing of leaking steam. The whole place was very dark with just a few beams of light coming through chinks in the side of the mill, as well as a glow from a few sawdust covered light bulbs burning here and there. Coming in from the outside, where the sun was hot and bright, you had the impression of falling into a well.

Before your eyes could become accustomed to the low light level there was the sound of a huge crash beside you, followed by another just above your head. A row of steam jacks had just thrown a log onto the head rig. I made my way through the murk, following the two others. As my eyes adapted I was able to make out the way we were going. First of all we went up to the log deck and then onto the one adjacent to it, where a group of men were pulling on slabs of timber, lining them up for Bill's gang saw. We then moved on and climbed a small staircase to what could only be the hog.

Glancing back over my shoulder I could see the whole of the head rig area from above, with the saw operators and of bearers working in a kind of strange silence. That is to say that it was not really silent at all, but the effect on your hearing was the same as if it had been. The inside of the mill was so noisy that you couldn't hear anything at all even if someone shouted at you from six feet away. By cupping your hands round someone's ear and bawling you had a chance. The only real way to communicate was by signs.

I turned and went through a small passage out into a staging about five feet square. On the far side was a chain bringing up the scrap from the mill and taking it to the burner. Crouching down in front of me were two millwrights, working on a heavy leather flap over the mouth of a hole in the floor, riveting up a tear. From a beam above hung down a long rope with a belt attached to its end. The whole of the platform was covered in blood!

Repairing the Hog

The normal operator was being taken to hospital for the third time. The basic trouble of the hog was that besides being a dangerous machine to work on, it made more noise than any other piece of equipment in the mill. Too much noise makes you careless, and this man had been careless for the third time.

The leather flap (a sort of "non return valve"), over the mouth of the hog had become worn and finally torn. A large chunk of wood had been spat back up, ripped aside the flap and removed one side of the worker's face. He was, in fact, very lucky. He wasn't killed, and he wasn't quite knocked out, so he didn't fall in the hog. Of course he was held by the belt attached to the beam so he couldn't fall in very far. He managed to undo the belt and get out to where someone could see the state he was in. It would have been no use shouting for help as none would have heard him.

It was the third time he'd been hurt working there and how he came back after seeing what it could do to you I have no idea. It must have been pride not to be licked by it. The two previous accidents had been less severe. He was in his early twenties and I believe had recently got married. The other men said that he was careless on the job. This was no doubt true but it was the very high continuous noise level that must have made him that way.

Well, I looked at the blood, I looked at the hog, I looked at the belt hanging from its rope and I looked at the blood again. The man with the mill boss saw me staring round and laughed. (You could hear him laugh with the hog lying idle). He lent over and shouted, "You have to leave the belt's rope long enough to be able to work. If you do slip into the hog it'll probably cut you off at about the knees, Slim, even with the safety belt. Pity you ain't smaller."

I put on the belt and they adjusted the length. It seemed to be horribly long. I hoped against hope that the millwrights would find something else wrong, but they seemed rather to be racing to finish the repair.

Just before I was left to start work I was told, "We can tell if you're not pulling enough by the amount of smoke coming out of the burner." I now found myself alone and looked into the chain. I saw that I'd have to pull more or less continuously to keep stuff from going on up to the burner. I grabbed my pickeroon and started the hog. Then, watching to keep out of a theoretical line of flight, I leant out and pulled off the first chunk.

For a moment I felt that I'd been shot in the ear. For a split second the whine of the hog had drowned out by a greedy, explosive "GRUMFF." I peered down and thought of my legs, and how dramatic it would be to return to college as an amputee. Well…I pulled the next chunk.

Soon my shoulder was aching from the sort of clawing action I had to use. I had to twist round and, using my right arm at full stretch, reach for each chunk on the chain and swing it across to feed the hog. This way I could keep my body back from the line of "backfire". Although a man came up with a pile of sawdust to sprinkle on the floor of the platform, it remained quite red, and one glance at it was enough to make me shrink back from the machine.

Suddenly someone tapped me on the shoulder. He pointed up in the air and pulled an imaginary whistle cord. It was time to eat. Now, the mill whistle was right above me where I stood on my platform, just on the other side of the roof, and although it could be heard all over the valley I couldn't hear it working on the hog!

I switched off and the noise dropped considerably. All that was left was a wild sort of screaming in my ears. I walked out of the mill as if in a daze towards the mess hall catching several of the others up as I went.

"Working on the hog?"

I looked at them blankly, the noise of the hog still ringing in my ears. From the way I squinted at them it was clear that I had not understood a word.

"Ears a-ringing huh? Don't worry, you'll get used to it in 'bout a week." They had heard about the accident and that I was the replacement.

After a few days we heard of another accident on a hog at a mill a few miles out of Dallas. I was asked, "Did you hear about the Philippino, down at Dallas?"

The man was obviously very keen to tell me, so I replied, "What Philippino?"

It seems that one of the power plant men was watching the hog fuel coming up the conveyor to the boilers and suddenly saw that the fuel had turned red. He stopped the conveyor and went to look for the Philippino. He wasn't there and he must have fallen in! The hog had ground him up in a flash and I was told, in great detail how, amongst the chips all they could find were bits of his boots. More gory details were added.

This little piece of news was told me to reassure me just as I was getting used to the job. To be truthful I never did like the hog and was afraid of it. It was less work to pull chunks off the chain up to the burner if you stood over the hog's mouth but I preferred to put up with getting tired and to keep back from it. The result was that as my shoulder became more and more tired I pulled less wood off into it. That led to the boss coming up to complain. He had noticed that the fire in the burner was getting suspiciously big, implying that I was "lying down on the job." After that I had to work harder, standing over the hog, hoping that the leather flap wouldn't rip again.

To my mind working on the hog was the worst job I had while at Valsetz.

With the chipper installed Otto's crew was ready to attack the drying kilns. These were a row of sheds in which green lumber is placed for up to a week to dry. The planks are stacked onto a sort of low wagon on rails and are then pushed into the kiln through the door. Each kiln could take some four wagons which means a lot of lumber. The inside of the building was lined with steam pipes all around the wagons and there were shutters in the roof to let out the steam.

Since all the wood going into the planing mill had to be dried and they certainly were not going to shut down the operation, the drying kilns could not be switched off entirely. So a few at a time were shut off and then demolished, new ones being built immediately by Otto's crew. This way the planing mill could keep running. Stan Henry's bull gang was to do the demolition, and I was, with relief, back on it.

Two high wooden dollies were made that could be wheeled into the empty kiln, just clearing the entrance lintel. The doors had been removed. Two "volunteers" were designated to climb up onto the top of the dolly and, armed with immensely long and heavy wrenches, were pushed into the still very hot kiln to dismantle the shutters in the ceiling.

The temperature outside was hovering around 105°F in the shade and perhaps 125°F in the sun, but the humidity was very low. Entering the kiln the temperature at the top of the dolly was near 150°F with a humidity of 100%; you could only just peer out of one eye at a time. Lower down it was cooler because the doors had been taken off, but if you stood up, as you had to, to reach the shutters and their bolts, you could neither open your eyes nor breathe.

You could make an interesting experiment lying on your back on the top of the dolly. If you raised your hand and then lowered it immediately you found your arm running in rivers of condensed steam. Taking a long breath and a last glimpse upwards into the clouds of vapour, you got to your feet with your eyes shut and started fumbling for the bolts. These had one and a half and two inch nuts to undo and were well rusted in. Getting the wrench onto the nut you dropped to your knees, where the temperature was lower and you could suck in a short breath between your lips, and then heaved away. It took three of us all morning to remove the shutters from one kiln.

The removal of the shutters let out nearly all the rest of the hot water vapour and it became easy to breathe again. The pipes were still very hot though, as I found when I tried to steady myself against one.

The next job was to take off the roof and two of us were given the task of sawing up old decking beams to length, to put across the rails inside the kiln. This way a truck could be backed in to be loaded with debris as it came down from above.

We set to, out in the broiling sun, with a crosscut saw. The old 4 x 12 beams had to be manoeuvred into position, but that done the rest was easy. It is amazing how fast a really sharp cross cut can cut through even a fairly thick piece of timber. In fact, once you had the knack, it was possible for just one man to do the sawing. We had become accustomed to the heat but were nevertheless a bit surprised to see that the temperature stood at 104° in the shade.

The roof consisted of four thicknesses of "one by" boards nailed together with tar paper between. Over the years this had become one solid tarry mass. We climbed up onto the roof and went over to the kiln being demolished. Looking down through the vents I could make out Stan Henry and his yellow packet of Peerless tobacco through the mist, some fifteen feet below. The first trucks were already backing in to pick up some odds and ends.

These trucks were bright red REOs belonging to an outside contracting company. One of the truck drivers was a young man who because of his swaggering about and conceited ways was sarcastically nicknamed "God." His pride came from his being a truck driver and his REO, a brand new one, was kept the most highly polished of the lot.

In a short while we members of the bull gang had cut through the outer layer of the roof's tarred boarding with axes and torn it back. Ripping off the vents we pushed cross cut saws through the openings and started sawing through the roof. When we had cut a little we attacked it with axes and steel bars, prizing off one layer at a time. The roof was laid on railroad rails running crosswise the kiln and we cut along close to them, so that we were always on solid structure. As the boards were peeled back they were thrown down into the truck below.

While this was going on the truck drivers retired outside at some distance from the kilns to sit and drink coffee.

The work seemed to go very slowly despite there being about six men working on the job. I was working with two others and we weren't laying around, but even then it was terribly slow work. What with the heat still coming up from the pipes, and the sun beating down, it was hot up there too. Surely, I thought, there must be a better way to get this stuff off. I turned to the other two.

"We're wasting our time doing it this way. Why don't we just cut out a slab between the rails, slide it on the rail so that it goes down into the truck? The others can help us push."

The two others decided to go along with it. They couldn't really have cared either way, as their $1.73 an hour would stay the same, but maybe they were happy to make the job easier too. We cut out a piece about five feet wide and eight feet long, using the crosscut and levering with the bars. It wasn't very big compared to the size of the roof but nevertheless a pretty hefty chunk. Then we got the others over to help push. This was harder to do than it looked as we all had to stoop down.

We all pushed, but the slab didn't slide at all. Instead it just started to tip. We all pushed like mad but it refused to slide and slowly rotated to become more or less vertical. Then, as we all looked on in horror, down it went with a tremendous crash!

Falling some eight feet it landed right on the truck's cab and continued down. We peered through the cloud of dust that it raised and saw that the cab and hood were flattened to the seat and engine block respectively. Both headlights were missing.

It was God's own beautiful truck! For a moment nobody said anything, but then I said, "I'd better go and tell Stan Henry."

We all went down and I went off to find Stan Henry, who was away elsewhere with another section of the bull gang. When I found him I told him what had happened and he went off to the mill office to see what would have to be done. I was sure that I had lost my job and skulked back slowly to the scene of the crime. So I'm afraid I missed out on something worth seeing.

Some of the men had gone to find the truck drivers and tell them what had taken place, but on the way invented a good story to say to God. It appears that they told him that he had won a certificate for the way he maintained his lovely REO and he was to come over to the kilns where it would be presented to him. He swallowed their story and almost burst with pride (which comes before a fall), and they all trooped back.

I'm not sure if he actually cried when he saw the state of his precious REO but his pride certainly took a fall!

Shortly after this Stan Henry arrived and surveyed the scene. He then called me over and I went to receive what I thought would be notice of being fired. All he said was, "That goldang truck was insured, but you'd better not do it again."

It wasn't long before we had dismantled two or three sheds. I was still up on the roof, taking off the boards...one by one! Next to me was another college student, Chuck, who was going to Lewis and Clark College and majoring in journalism. He was sawing a slot in the roof with a cross cut saw when suddenly the whole roof gave way.

To my horror I saw the saw's teeth rotate upwards as Chuck fell right across it. As he rolled over I could see that he was grabbing his left thigh and that blood was coming out through his trouser leg.

The roof was still attached in part, being hung up on either some of the pipes or being supported by a truck underneath. Anyway, I was able to leap down to where he lay and look at his leg. Now the teeth of a cross cut saw are long and they appeared to have gone right in. It's strange, but right away came back to me something I'd heard about pressure points, probably from listening to someone giving first aid instruction during the war. I remembered that there was one on the inside of the thigh so I searched around for it with my thumb. Blood seemed to be pouring out all over the place. At last I found that by pushing in a certain place the flow was cut to practically nothing. While I bore down with both hands and somebody made him as comfortable as possible a third went off to find the company doctor. Chuck said that it hurt a lot and looked very pale under his suntan.

While I was secretly pleased with my remembering a bit of what I'd either heard or perhaps learnt about First Aid (it would have been in basic Boy Scout training, I would expect), I was wondering what was going to happen in about twenty minutes time if the doctor didn't come. I also remembered that every fifteen or twenty minutes you had to let the blood flow again or else the limb could die. My two thumbs, pressed down into his leg in a pool of coagulating blood were getting very tired, but as I knew next to nothing about applying a tourniquet I had to go on pushing. Then the doctor arrived.

He immediately saw that the blood was coming out from a big vein and not an artery, so it was not quite so dangerous after all. I think he cut off the trouser leg and applied bandages. Chuck was looking weaker and weaker. Then the "ambulance" arrived.

It was not the sort of deluxe thing you see in a city but a "crummy," as used for taking the loggers out to into the woods. This was a four wheel drive truck with a wooden compartment built on the back. It was equipped with two way radio.

Chuck was eased onto a stretcher and carefully placed in the back of the crummy. It was a very painful ride for him, as we heard over the radio. It took them the best part of an hour just to get to Falls City, because to minimize the jolting they didn't dare go too fast. From there to the hospital in Dallas it must have been easier on him.

The next day we drove out over to the hospital to see him. The colour had returned to his face and he was in bed convalescing. I don't remember if he recovered sufficiently to return for work at Valsetz again that summer or not.

In some parts around the mill where we were replacing the old timber decking by a gravel fill it was necessary to build a wooden retaining wall. Down by the railroad this was quite a lot of fun for the gang, as after setting up the piles in place we could sit down in the sun while the railroad's steam crane drove them in, using a massive steam pile driver at the end of its jib. With each blow they went down a couple of feet into the soft marshy soil. When we went to fetch more piles we rode on the front of the crane as it chuffed slowly along the track. High above us, like a lord, stood the driver surrounded by a maze of levers and pistons, with steam hissing everywhere, silhouetted against the firebox door.

The Valley & Siletz RR, steam crane

The crane was a big one, self propelled on eight wheels and with a long lattice jib. It was responsible for the switching of railroad cars around the head rig side of the mill where the track would not support the weight of a road locomotive. It was also, as in this case, used to help with millwright work within the reach of its jib. Its real reason for existence though was as a wreck crane being capable of picking up a standard freight car. It fitted in very well with the 1920's decor of Valsetz, along with the two road locomotives used to bring the trains up to and out from the town. These engines were two "Mikado" 2-8-2s, black and powerful. Most of these trains, I was told, were made up mainly of "foreign" freight cars which had to be loaded and taken away within four days to avoid the company having to pay extra money.

I was intrigued to hear of foreign cars and wondered where they could have come from. Canada most probably or perhaps even Mexico, where it's too dry to grow Douglas fir.

The loading bays ran along by the planing mill and one evening I went over to it to see where these foreigners came from. Well, there was one solitary Canadian Pacific and all the rest were from the U.S.A.: Southern Pacific, U.P., Milwaukee Road, Nickel Plate and Frisco. I mentioned to Old George that all I had found was one foreign car and he laughed. The company railroad, the Valley and Siletz joined the Southern Pacific at Independence down on the Willamette and all freight cars not belonging to the S.P. were "foreign." The Nickel Plate Route and Frisco didn't sound very un-American to me. I was disappointed.

Some of the pile driving had to be done at quite a way from the railroad track, up in between the planing mill and the dry kilns. Since I had found the job so agreeable and easy I was glad to be told to go there one morning, to start on the job of laying in a length of low retaining wall. The piles were to be simply the old railroad rails that had already been used for the roof structure of the dismantled dry kilns. These were much easier to handle than the heavy wooden piling that we'd used up to then.

So the next morning there I was, waiting for an easy day's labour to begin. Stan Henry told us that the truck had gone to get the pile driver. I was surprised to see that there were six of us, as we'd been only four before. We found out why we were six when the truck arrived and we looked at each other in disbelief. The "pile driver" looked like a guillotine with a heavy weight replacing the blade. A stout rope led up from the weight and over a pulley and out to where we could tail on and pull it up.

The truck bed was tipped until the pile driver slipped back and then driven forward until it dropped off. We dragged it over into place and raised the first rail into position. Then with five of us pulling back we raised the weight, a very easy thing to do as we were fit and the weight weighed not much over one hundred pounds. In fact, with us all not knowing how much effort would be required it shot up to the top of the frame. Letting it go it went down onto the head of the rail, driving it in with a satisfying bang. Having to pull back and then let go was quite enjoyable.

In the sun it was hot but with a light wind quite supportable. The weight clanked up and down on the top of one rail after another. The only trouble was that it seemed to take a very long time to drive the rail right down. They had to be driven in ten feet or more and up in this part of the mill the ground was much harder than down by the lake.

After three hours we were getting pretty tired, especially as the sun was rising to its zenith. At noon we were all fed up with the damn pile-driver. The only good thing in it for me was that we were to work four hours overtime per day until all the piles were in. That afternoon four extra men came to join the gang and we worked until nine o'clock that evening. Stan Henry had been told to get the bulkhead in fast as the trucks bringing the gravel would be arriving on the Saturday and it was already Wednesday. Thursday we worked all day but in the evening still had a long way to go. Then on Friday morning, for the first time that summer, it started to rain and it cooled off a bit. By the end of another day's work we had driven all the remaining piles in part way, so that the bulkhead could be put in and the gravel poured. The final driving down of the piles would be done later.

The trucks were already arriving to unload and the D.8 bulldozer was leveling the ground on the far side of the planing mill. We worked on, the rain getting harder and it really seemed to be settling in. Valsetz looked much different in the rain. The wooden walkways round the bunkhouses, instead of being a pleasant place to sit, with your legs dangling over the edge, had become slippery and wet. Blackie had lit the fire in the cabin and we hurried down to eat in the mess hall.

In the afternoon it was really pouring and I began to get soaked. Most of the men had oilskin rain gear, but my $15 safety boots were all I had in the way of real work clothes. The rain began to come down harder and harder.

Suddenly a pickup arrived at full tilt, windshield wipers going full speed. It was Brownjohn in person.

"Stan Henry, get all your men over to where they're laying the gravel. Have them all take picks and shovels."

As soon as we got over there we saw a lake forming everywhere. The D.8 had nicked the main water line into the town, a huge main leading down from a dam up above Valsetz. Someone had gone up to shut off the pipe but meanwhile water was boiling up in the centre of a big pool. We stood watching and after a few minutes the pool went off the boil. Our job was to go into the pool and dig out the broken pipe so that it could be fixed before the whistle blew on Monday morning. The pile driving was forgotten.

Of course, the rain became even heavier. We waded into the pool and with water up to our thighs began to shovel out the high quality gravel that had only just been dumped in. By evening I was absolutely soaked to the skin. The water had receded somewhat but the rain continued.

When I got back to the bunkhouse Blackie was just taking off his oil slicks and hanging them up to drain. I had to take off every stitch I had on and put on my good trousers before going off to eat. After the meal I was presented with a problem, as we were to go back to work that evening and I had only the one set of work clothes, still soaked. As I started to put the wet things back on someone in the room took pity on me,

"Say, English, why don't you take that old pair of slicks from off the wall. They're not much but at least they're not wet."

Normally, of course, you wear your normal work clothes under oilskins. The only thing was that the only thing I had two of was a spare work shirt, so I put that on and climbed in. The oilskins felt cold and damp against my bare lower parts, but not as bad as the cold wet jeans. I went out into the rain and back to the job. It was, despite a sort of naked feeling, much more comfortable working in something waterproof. I shoveled away with energy, the slicks, much to large for me, flapping back and forth.

All of a sudden I had a terrible sensation. A cold breeze was coming in at the seat of the trousers.

"Jesus Christ! The goddam rotten old things have ripped up the seat!" These were my immediate thoughts, but luckily I didn't express my feelings out loud. I became even more aware that I had nothing on underneath. It began to seem like a nightmare, but nobody had noticed. Luckily they all had their heads down in the rain.

Then I realized to my horror that I couldn't leave as it would mean walking away from the rest of the gang. If anyone found out that English worked in old oilskins split up the back, with nothing on underneath it would be worse than the REO truck incident.

But if I couldn't leave I couldn't stop working and if I dug I would have to bend down. However I found that by keeping at the right angle to the little wind that there was and hardly leaning on the shovel my predicament was not obvious. I then began to move slowly between each shovelful, off to the side sufficiently to have no one behind me. Then, shoveling as little as possible I worked in the rain waiting for night to fall.

When at last we stopped for the night I made sure that I was the last person to walk away from the job and back to the bunkhouses. Over an inch of rain had fallen that afternoon and evening.

Monday morning the weather was hot and fine again. The pipe had been repaired and gravel bulldozed in again. After a couple more days of fruitless banging with the hand pile-driver a millwright came over and cut the tops off the parts of rail that were still sticking up above road level.

On and off throughout the summer, whenever there was a lull in work for the bull gang, other jobs were found to keep us busy. These were often unpleasant ones chosen to enrich our small amount of experience. They included hauling garbage with Peterson in the heat of the day and rebuilding the septic tanks of the outlying houses. Both of these tasks had been imposed on the company by the State health authorities, I believe.

The first of these was perhaps because an outside contractor who usually collected the garbage was asking too much and Peterson offered to take the job over. All I remember was how ripe the contents were. Since the cans had been standing in the sun for several days and their bottoms were sufficiently corroded that a powerful liquid ran out when you lifted them up, the overall effect can easily be imagined.

The septic tank job had its funny moments. It must be remembered that the loggers considered themselves the cream of the workers at Valsetz, probably correctly. Below them came the sliver-pickers and way below them the bull gang. Their superior attitude was certainly felt by we members of the gang. So one day we were happy to get our own back, when we were sent out to re-do the septic tank at a logger's house. It was quite apparent to the logger's wife that we were poor specimens physically, when she saw our feeble muscles and our work rate. I don't remember if it got to as far as making funny remarks, but certainly we were made to feel very inferior. Of course there was nothing we could do but keep on going.

Revenge came in a most unexpected form as just as we disconnected the house's outlet pipe in order to run it into the new tank, we were recalled back to do some urgent job at the mill. We didn't manage to get back to hook up their plumbing for four days! When we did get back we noticed that the logger's wife stayed indoors.

On the gang for most of the summer were two brothers, sons of a Protestant minister somewhere up near Portland, I think. One of these boys, Sam, was big and fat and sunburned easily. His brother seemed to be much the more "spiritual" of the two. He winced, at least inwardly, at the foul language in common use at Valsetz, especially when it was spoken by a woman. For this reason language seemed to get noticeably worse when he was around. He wore a sort of khaki twill uniform and looked rather like a laundry delivery man. I believe that he was in a seminary somewhere and had been educated to have horror of manual work. He wasn't a bad mixer, it was just that Valsetz was hardly his element and in fact, in retrospect, it is amazing that he ever came to work there.

He left before the end of the summer, after a story of a misfortune of his got around. Of course, it might just as well have been me and my split oilskins.

We had been digging holes in everyone's gardens, eight feet long by six wide, some four or five feet deep. These were then lined with cedar planks, with a cedar baffle across. They were the new septic tanks demanded by the Polk County Health Department. We had, as often as not, a hole each to dig. Sam's brother was given one all alone, where? At the back of a logger's house of course. His hole apparently grew at a pathetically slow rate. The poor lad was not up to the job, and the Valsetz soil, typical of the region was hard with lots of rocks and stones in it, as we had earlier discovered. He had worked for perhaps three days on his hole with his already slow work rate made even slower by the logger's wife. She came out to be entertained by him and this embarrassment made him more feel more awkward than ever. He continued to chip away under a barrage of disparaging remarks, down in his hole with the hot sun beating down.

That evening she told the rest of the proceedings to her highly amused husband when he returned from the woods. He then relayed her story to all and sundry with great relish and some detail. I never heard the minister's son's version of it since from that day I never saw him again.

Apparently, as he was throwing tiny amounts of soil up out of the hole he heard her say,

"You ain't never gonna get the goddamn thing done by yourself. I'll pick and you shovel!"

To his dismay, (and perhaps the story had been a little exaggerated by the time it reached me) he saw her strip to the waist and leap down into the pit with him. Trying not to hear the constant stream of profanity coming from her lips he had to shovel like mad and make sure he was not hit by either her swinging pick or breasts! That was the story, and I mused over what I would have done in such a situation.

One afternoon Stan Henry was told by Brownjohn to go out to his house and get out a tree that had grown too large and was giving too much shade. Stan Henry came up to me and with a look rather like a schoolboy up to mischief, asked me if I would like to see how expert he was in the use of dynamite. So we got into his old Dodge and, picking up hammer, nails and some boards, drove out to the private residence of the Superintendent. Stan said that he'd blow the tree with three sticks.

The house was a pleasant white frame single story place. I was told to start nailing and boarding up the windows. The tree to be blown was about five feet away from the nearest window. I sawed and hammered away while Stan Henry walked round the tree prodding between the roots. It didn't take long to get the windows boarded up, so I was soon at work on the main part of the job, digging down between the roots to find the right place to put each stick of dynamite.

We must have kept on working after the mill had quit for the day, because I remember very clearly the sight of a millwright and his girl friend strolling up along the valley road towards me. From down in my hole they looked like any other couple and I didn't pay much attention. I went back to my sapping operation. But when I looked up again I realized that it was a couple unique in Valsetz. It was Tiny, the seven foot tall waitress and her boyfriend, a hefty millwright who topped her by a couple of inches! I remember how I watched them going on up the road and thinking how normal they looked when there wasn't anyone round to compare them with. It seemed a shame that they should be so isolated from the rest of the world just because they were giants.

The millwrights had an ex-army Dodge truck, with the doors removed, that this giant could drive. It was practically impossible for him to get both legs into the cab and he drove with his left leg hanging out. Unfortunately he used to suffer from occasional epileptic fits which were quite terrifying to witness. He wasn't supposed to drink alcohol but, being lonely, I think he did. This apparently increased his chances of having an attack. He shouldn't really have been a truck driver but he was, and one day had an attack while backing the Dodge up to the green chain. He half fell out of the truck while it bashed into one of the roof supports. The truck in reverse gear continued to spin its wheels backwards throughout it all, threatening to bring down the roof on top of everyone. After it was over a worker switched of the engine. He didn't stop driving just because of this incident though.

A few minutes before Stan Henry was ready to blow the tree we heard the sound of a car coming along fast from the direction of Valsetz. We could soon see it coming, bucking and jumping from one side of the road to the other, missing half the holes and hitting the other fifty percent head on. Soon you could see that it was painted bright yellow, its colour showing up clearly against the cloud of white dust trailing behind it. It got closer very quickly and Stan Henry sighed. It was Brownjohn who had just learnt that his tree was about to be removed by dynamite.

Stan Henry stood unabashed before Brownjohn as the latter read him up one side and down the other. They then agreed to use a bulldozer instead of explosives. Stan Henry did try to convince his superior that all would be safe and pointed to the boarded up windows. Brownjohn was not amused. The boards had been put up with eight penny nails, whose traces would remain on the window frames when the boards themselves were removed.

The next day I spent excavating under the tree. Later a bulldozer came out from the mill and after cutting off some of the roots we got the thing out.

In the valley the company was clearing out bush to add to the pasture area for their cattle. This to Stan Henry's joy, meant blowing stumps. Sitting on the step outside the bunkhouse drinking a well earned beer, we would hear the thuds of dynamite going off. When the stumps were blown, scattered round the land in a tangle of huge dismembered black claws, Stan Henry, by the cunning placement of more explosives, blew them together into one big pile for burning. Despite his unlucky adventure with the drainage ditch he was certainly a master in the use of dynamite.

Stan Henry was an institution at Valsetz, having taken part in its construction in 1919. By the 1950's when he was really in a sort of retirement he was still "playing" with dynamite and running the bull gang. I recall that once when, with the help of the steam crane, we were putting in a large lumber storage deck, just across from the lumber slide by the blacksmiths' shop. The deck was made up of tree trunks resting on piles, each trunk being about forty feet long. For three of us to manoeuvre them into position was a delicate operation, even with the help of the steam crane. By pushing on the end of the trunk while the crane held it up in the air it was possible to start it to rotate. As it swung round, it had to be positioned by the crane so that it dropped neatly into place. The crane driver was obviously an artist!

With the crane retreating up the track to get another trunk we had a moments relaxation. Stan Henry, his chin, neck and undershirt yellow with chewing tobacco juice, nudged me and pulled out his wallet. With a knowing look he extracted a thick packet of pornographic photographs to show us. As a callow youth I was not only both interested and shocked, but also greatly impressed by his delight in them, what with him being over seventy years old.

He went on to tell us how, when he got married, he took his young bride with him to make a last farewell visit to all the brothels that he knew. According to him the girls all flocked around him as he entered each one, whereupon he presented them to his wife, who was understandably embarrassed.

"But look," he said to her, "what pleasures I am giving up for you."

Until that spring when he had had a heart attack Stan Henry had been a heavy drinker, and I noticed that while working on the bull gang he still carried a flask of whiskey in his hip pocket. During the previous winter the whole gang had got drunk while shoveling snow from off the mill's roofs. They had had a huge snowball fight and then thrown the snow down on the millworkers below.

But even after his heart attack Stan Henry was amongst the strongest men at Valsetz, along with Otto, Peterson and some of the loggers.

The first weekend in September I went up to Portland. I had scratched my knee and done nothing about it. It had become infected with streptococci and lots of little bumps were coming up and weeping. I soon had it over the back of my hands too. I went to see a doctor, since the infection was spreading quickly and I was starting to run a fever. To my surprise he sent me down to pass the weekend in hospital. It was quite a come down to have worked all summer at Valsetz and then to end up in hospital because of a bug! I was off work for a week and when I returned to the mill it was for only one more week before I had to go back to college.

Rather than going back to work on the bull gang, I worked on the green chain as marker, a job that could qualify me as a genuine sliverpicker.

At last autumn and with it college had arrived. I had only to pack my bag, say "so long" to everyone, collect my last paycheck and hitch-hike back to the big city.

Having worked at Valsetz one summer I considered myself well qualified to work there again the following year. So when school finished in 1952 I went down to Falls City on the bus with a college friend. We then hitch-hiked over into Valsetz. Once again I walked up to the superintendent's office to ask for a job. Just as before Brown-john came to the door, but when I asked if I could work there he just said "Nope," turned his back on me and went back in.

I don't know, and never will know, if it was because they had finished remodelling the mill, or whether he remembered the damage I'd done the year before. Anyway we had to leave, so seeing a logger about to drive out of town I asked him if he could take us as far as Falls City.

This he did, thus providing a farewell episode about Valsetz. He had a new Chevrolet with fluid drive and it was clear that he was very proud of it. I remember saying that fluid drive was all very nice, but that if you lost the brakes you couldn't use the engine for braking. "Why not?" he said, as we shot over a ridge and started a breakneck descent towards Falls City, "You can always put it into reverse."

And he did.

We picked ourselves up from the floor of the car and continued on down. From there we hitched back to Portland.

APPENDIX 1: THREE MORE SHORT ANECDOTES

1. Driving the dump truck.

One of the more unusual aspects of driving the dump truck was that it had a leak in its hydraulic system and the brakes could suddenly fail at any moment. It would then have to be driven with no brakes for the rest of the day.

They failed on me once just as I started down a steep ramp that led under the mill's main log deck. I pushed in the clutch, revved the engine up to maximum in neutral and rammed it in low gear. Very luckily it went in and with a frightening shudder we slowed down sufficiently for me to steer round the posts holding up the deck. I was given a few questioning looks as I roared out to the other side of the deck. It was all over in a couple of seconds but it really made me think. I could have hit one of the pillars and I had a full load of gravel just behind me! The lesson learnt was, "DON'T RELY ON YOUR BRAKES," and from then on I always engaged compound low before starting down the ramp, even if the brakes were working.

With no brakes it was an interesting process backing round on to a traverser (also with no brakes) and across into the dry kilns that were being taken down. Nobody was ever watching so I was able to take my time, and I finally became really proficient.

All this was spoilt though, when one day after dumping a load I forgot to lower the bed and was seen driving happily along—by Brown-john!

No wonder I was not hired the following year.

2. Two 'Unfortunates'.

The noise level in parts of the mill was, as has been noted, extremely high, yet none of the mill-workers wore any ear-protectors. The result was, for a certain number of men, premature deafness and (as was pointed out to me later) a return to childlike behaviour.

In the canteen I sat with Otto on my right and an 'unfortunate' on my left. This man practically never spoke but if I could hardly talk to him I could still watch him with amazement as he smothered all his food with Tabasco sauce—including apple pie! I managed to ask him why did he do it? The reply, "Gives it a kick!"

One day he didn't turn up. He had got mad at, or tired of, Valsetz, and had been seen walking off down the railroad track out of town. Nobody expressed surprise at his literally walking off, but they did when they found out that he had not bothered to go to the mill office to collect his pay.

Systematically another 'unfortunate', after his meal, would stop by the canteen doorway to grab a pile of toothpicks and then proceed to use them to prod and dig inside his ears!

So much for the good old days!

3. A case of dynamite.

Stan Henry both loved dynamite and chewed "Peerless" tobacco. Not wishing to spit in public, part of the "Peerless" juice would descend down his chin to dye his undershirt. I didn't find this a very attractive sight, perhaps because I neither smoked nor chewed.

One day I was down in a ditch when Stan offered me a chew. Not unnaturally I refused. He kept on insisting and I kept on refusing until finally he gave up, remarking that what he was offering me wasn't really tobacco at all—it was a piece of dynamite!

I often wish that I'd fallen for his joke. Imagine being able to relate, truthfully, how out working in the Wild West, you'd chewed dynamite!

APPENDIX 2: STAN HENRY AND THE CONCORDE

The prototype Concorde supersonic airliner first flew on 2nd March 1969 and of course was initially limited to subsonic flight. Little by little the so-called flight envelope was extended and Mach 2 was reached for the first time in November 1970.

The aircraft's behaviour in the designed cruise conditions seemed excellent until low incidence flight was investigated. This led to loud bangs as all four engines surged and stopped and the crew, to their surprise, found themselves flying a supersonic glider! With no more thrust they obviously slowed down, and on increasing incidence the four engines re-lit.

This sort of behaviour was certainly inadmissible on a certificated civil airliner and a solution had to be found in the shortest possible time…if, in fact, there was one.

It had been a degradation of the airflow round the inboard wing's leading edge that had led to the surging, and the remedy was to modify the shape of this leading edge to improve the quality of the flow at low incidence.

In 1970 we had no theoretical means to calculate the flow adjacent to this part of the wing. So I, being the lucky man designated to improve the shape, had to imagine what sort of new geometry might work.

We had been forewarned about the possibility of a problem shortly before the flight tests. Wind tunnel testing had shown that there was a potential problem, and I had drawn up a family of progressively blunter wing leading edges. It was now urgent to define them precisely, so that models could be manufactured for more wind tunnel tests.

There was no time to work up a mathematical definition and the only solution seemed to be to do it on the drawing board. This was not going to be easy as the shapes had to be drawn with great accuracy and the wing's inboard leading edge was some 50 feet long!

I suddenly thought back to working at Valsetz with Stan Henry.

It wasn't mentioned in the1963 text, but one day the Bull Gang had been set to lay out a short spur of railroad track. Two things I remember very well, firstly how to spike down railroad track with a gandy-dancer's hammer, using the thick side of the head to start the spike and then the thin one to finish the job. I was told in no uncertain terms of the dire consequences if I missed the spike and dented the rail!

The second thing that I learnt was the amazing precision that one can obtain by eye, as follows:

The rails had been put roughly in place and had been bolted together, with the spur going off in a gradual curve. The Bull Gang's job was to slew the line so that the curve was absolutely smooth and progressive, and then to spike it down.

Stan Henry stood at the beginning of the spur, squinting along the rail. At his command we all heaved on our bars as hard as we could and it moved perhaps a quarter of an inch.

When it was almost slewed into place Stan Henry called out, "Come here English!" (or had my name been upgraded to "Slim?") He knew that I was a college boy and so was in great need to be educated.

"What do you think of that?" he asked me, and I looked along the rail to see it slowly and progressively entering into its curve. "Just see what you can do by eye." I was really impressed.

Then to my surprise I heard, "Get back on the bar!" So back I went to the others to heave again. We leant on our bars and heaved, with the result that the rail moved a fraction of an inch. I heard Stan Henry call "Come and have another look." So I squinted along the rail again. The curve had been beautifully smooth before, but this now it was perfect!

Remembering my lesson of some twenty years earlier I laid out sections of the wing on the drawing board, at full size, in such a manner that it looked as if I was Stan Henry squinting along the wing's leading edge. Then, using long flexible plastic splines, I was able to adjust the shape of the sections so that the profile ran smoothly all along its fifty foot length. Despite the large changes of leading edge radius and droop, as well as the need to blend in smoothly with the rest of the wing before reaching the front wing spar the whole job turned out well. From one end to the other the modified profiles were defined to a precision of about half a millimetre!

From the drawings models were made for testing in the supersonic wind tunnel at Modane, in the Alps, and to everyone's relief a satisfactory solution seemed to have been found.

The prototype was modified (a really major industrial operation) and flown to check the new shape. I well remember waiting apprehensively for its landing. It finally returned, taxied in and the door opened. The flight engineer, M. Henri Perrier, appeared, with a huge smile on his face!

I can visualize him still. For me it was a moment of both joy and relief, an certainly a highlight in my aerodynamic career.

www.ingramcontent.com/pod-product-compliance
Lightning Source LLC
Chambersburg PA
CBHW020437030426
42337CB00014B/1303